Bird-Eating Spiders

by Claire Archer

www.abdopublishing.com

Published by Abdo Kids, a division of ABDO, PO Box 398166, Minneapolis, Minnesota 55439.

Copyright © 2015 by Abdo Consulting Group, Inc. International copyrights reserved in all countries. No part of this book may be reproduced in any form without written permission from the publisher.

Printed in the United States of America, North Mankato, Minnesota.

052014

092014

THIS BOOK CONTAINS RECYCLED MATERIALS

Photo Credits: Animals Animals, Glow Images, Minden Pictures, Science Source, Shutterstock, © nikoretro p. 5/ CC-BY-SA-2.0

Production Contributors: Teddy Borth, Jennie Forsberg, Grace Hansen

Design Contributors: Candice Keimig, Laura Rask, Dorothy Toth

Library of Congress Control Number: 2013952992

Cataloging-in-Publication Data

Archer, Claire.

 Bird-eating spiders / Claire Archer.

   p. cm. -- (Spiders)

ISBN 978-1-62970-071-7 (lib. bdg.)

Includes bibliographical references and index.

1. Bird-eating spiders--Juvenile literature. I. Title.

595.4--dc23

                  2013952992

Table of Contents

Bird-Eating Spiders

Bird-eating spiders live in **swampy** places. They live in forests too.

4

Bird-eating spiders usually live in **burrows**. Some will live under plants and branches.

Bird-eating spiders

are a type of tarantula.

Tarantulas are big spiders.

9

The largest spider on Earth
is a bird-eater. It is called
the goliath bird-eating spider.

11

Bird-eaters have eight legs and eight eyes. Their bodies are covered in thick hair.

13

Bird-eaters are usually brown or black. Some are colorful.

14

Food

Bird-eating spiders sometimes eat birds. This is how they got their name.

It is **rare** for bird-eaters to eat birds. They eat insects and other spiders. They eat frogs, lizards, and snakes too.

Baby Bird-Eating Spiders

Female bird-eaters lay eggs. After they hatch, babies usually stay near their mothers. Soon they are on their own.

20

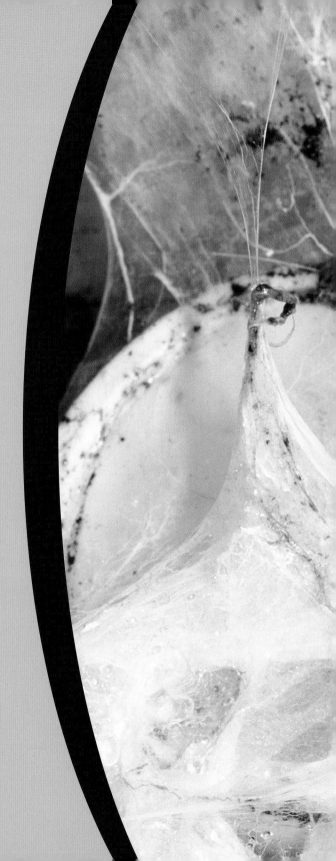

More Facts

- Female bird-eating spiders can live for 25 years.

- Bird-eaters have bad eyesight. This is because they do not have to rely on eyesight for hunting.

- Bird-eaters rely on feeling for vibrations when hunting.

- One defense of the bird-eater is to flick its hairs at the **predator**. Its hairs will irritate the skin or eyes.

Glossary

burrow – an animal's underground home.

predator – an animal that lives by eating other animals.

rare – not usual.

swampy – swamp-like. A swamp is wet land that is filled with trees and/or other plants.

tarantula – a large, hairy spider.

Index

abdokids.com

Use this code to log on to abdokids.com and access crafts, games, videos and more!

Abdo Kids Code:
SBK0717